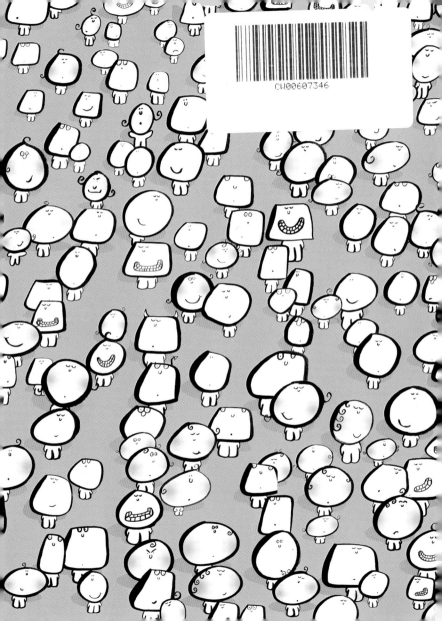

dads

with Vimrod

dads

life is a journey
between
the
fridge
and the
sofa

Vimrod by Lisa Swerling and Ralph Lazar

HarperCollins*Publishers*

dads are the best

(banks)

a **dad's** body is built
to hunt **mammoths**
and to **watch football.**

if there are no mammoths left
to hunt, it is fully within his rights
to watch football.

all the time.

hickory-dickory-
dock, the mouse
ran up the
clock,
where it got
caught in a
trap laid by
my dad.

my dad is in the ant harvesting business and he's made millions (of ants, that is).

sometimes being
an old fart is quite

exhausting

my dad snores in

fourteen

different

languages

dad,
you're the
sheriffest
sheriff
in the West.

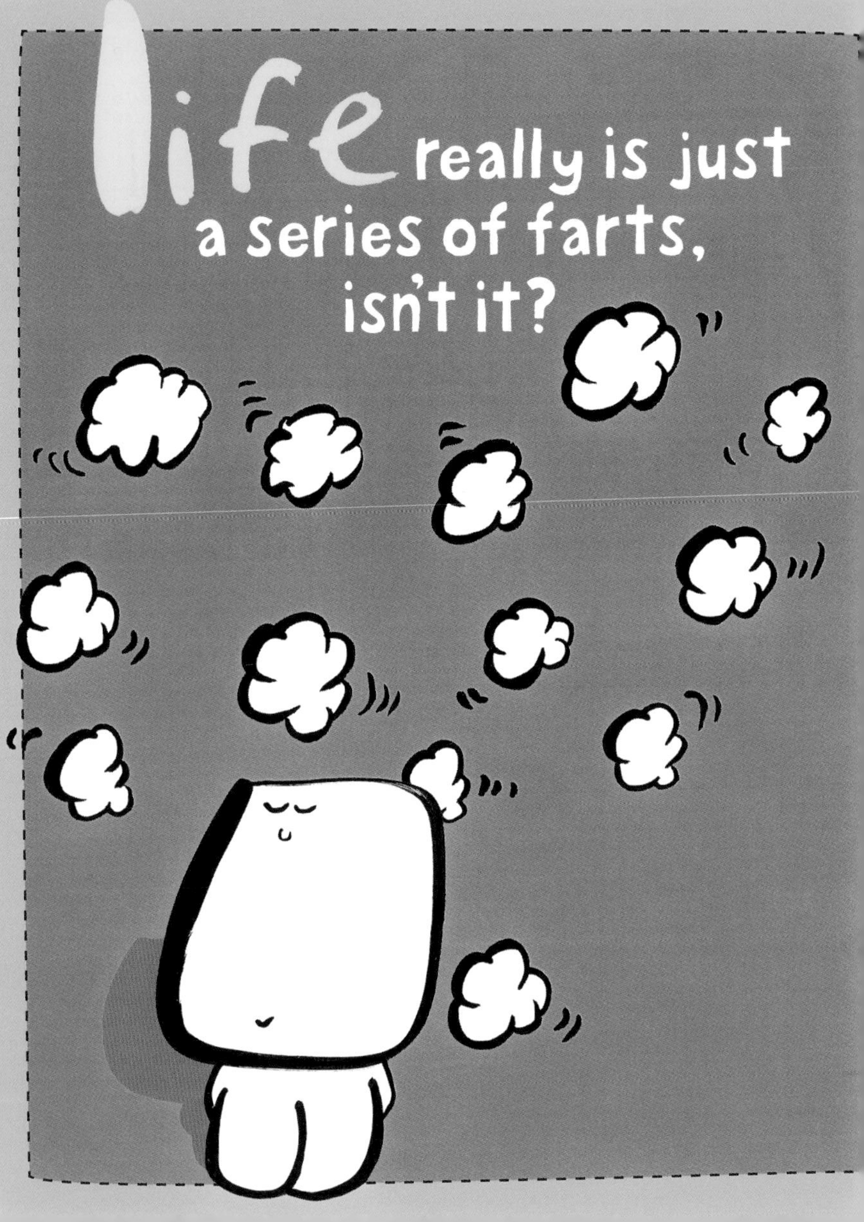
life really is just
a series of farts,
isn't it?

a while back, dads were given a choice:

evolve or watch football.

224,
225,
226...

the rest is history.

beware of the entrances to pubs.

one minute

you're innocently walking by, the **next** you're sucked in and forced to have a pint.

well what kind of a dad are you?

if
at first
you don't succeed,

give up and go to the pub.

listen to
your elders

(except if
they are
wrong)

it is so **complicated** being a **dad**.

which beer to drink?
which team to support?
when to not fart?

are two of the UK's most familiar
graphic artists. Through their company
Last Lemon they have spawned a catwalk
of popular cartoon characters, which
includes Harold's Planet, The Brainwaves,
Blessthischick and, of course, Vimrod.

Writers, artists and designers, they are
married with two children, and spend
their time between London and various
beaches on the Indian Ocean.

HarperCollins*Publishers*

77–85 Fulham Palace Road, Hammersmith, London W6 8JB

www.harpercollins.co.uk

Published by HarperCollins*Publishers* 2007

1

A catalogue record for this book is available from the British Library

ISBN-13 978 0 00 724208 5

Set in Bokka
Printed and bound in Italy by Lego SpA

other titles in the **Vimrod** collection:

(watch
this
space)

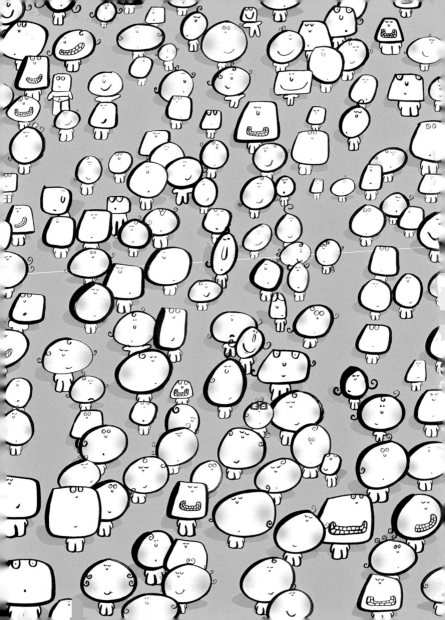